Adwords
"Made Easy"
for Small
Business Owners

Eoin O'Leary

DEDICATION

To my Partner, Mary

LEGAL NOTICES

CONTENTS

Foreword

What this book is

This book answers many of the questions I get asked about Google™ AdWords™. How AdWords work, what use might AdWords be to a business and how to use them to make more profit for your business.

What this book is not

This book is not a "how to" guide for Google Adwords. However I do provide links to the best "how to" information you can get, directly from Google™.

It's free to access and is used by Adwords experts to gain certification from Google™. You will find them in the resources section.

Introduction

Google AdWords is a popular advertising product developed by Google inc. and is rapidly becoming an essential part of Digital Marketing.

This is mainly because Google AdWords can be up and running very quickly, there is no waiting months before seeing results.

Also, so many people are connected to the Internet using computers, tablet computers or smart phones. As a business owner using Google AdWords, you will be able to reach these people, no matter what method they use to access the Internet and no matter where they may be, Local, National or International.

It's also possible to target people who are more likely to buy from you, unlike traditional advertising where an advert is placed for everyone to see a properly constructed Google advert only gets seen by people that will probably be interested in what you have to offer.

Well targeted Google AdWords ads are far cheaper compared to traditional adverts and with proper testing, some businesses find that not only can they get far better Return On the advertising investment, they can actually use the Google AdWords reports to grow their business in directions they had not know opportunities existed.

Google AdWords, Some History

Google AdWords™ are basically an advertising product developed by Google inc. and it is the company's main source of revenue today. Google reported revenues of US$10.65 billion for the quarter ended March 31, 2012.
(http://investor.google.com/earnings/2012/Q1_google_earnings.html), most of which was related to income from business spending on Google Adwords.

NOTE: This should be your first hint to the fact that despite what some people say, Google Adwords do make a good return on investment for advertisers. Business Owners & CEO's don't give anyone US$10.65 billion without getting something in return.

Google's AdWords are managed by a whole division and this is housed in Ann Arbor in Michigan – it is Google's 3rd largest facility besides its headquarters in California and its office in New York.

Bill Gross from a company called *Idealab* came up with the original idea. Google tried to buy the *"idea"*, they could not reach an agreement, and so Google went ahead and established AdWords™ in 2000.

Google AdWords followed Bill Gross' model to some extent, but Google claimed it was a different idea. *IdeaLab* sued Google and it was settled out of court.

When Google AdWords was originally launched, advertisers paid a fixed monthly amount to Google and Google would then set up and manage their advertising campaign.

However, the company had to change this strategy to accommodate small businesses and those who wanted to manage their own campaigns – this led to the establishment of AdWords™ self-service portal, that we use today.

Adwords has gone beyond just advertising in their own Search Engine results, they now have access to hundreds of thousands of high-quality websites, news pages, and blogs that partner with Google to display AdWords ads.

How Google AdWords Works

Google AdWords works on an auction-based system that allows advertisers to bid on "key words" that people use, when they are using the Google Search Engine and to place Google Adverts on Google's Partner Sites. The company makes its billions by charging its advertisers, every time a visitor clicks on the advertisers advert.

Google is all about *relevancy*. If an advert receives few clicks meaning that consumers do not find the advert particularly relevant to the search they have performed, Google downgrades it in its sponsored link ranking system.

This is helps ensure that the most relevant adverts appear most frequently. This makes good commercial sense, for Google and Advertisers.

Advertisers can choose to have their adverts displayed on high traffic Web sites or they can have these adverts on the far right side of the screen when a Google search results page is displayed.

Ads on specific Web sites are called *'Placement Specific Adverts'* and the adverts that are found on the far right side of the screen are called *'Keyword Targeted Adverts.'*

Placement Specific Adverts are normally based on the number of *"impressions"* the advert gets, which is the number of times the advert appears on a web site.

Keyword Targeted Adverts are charged on a pay-per-click basis, which is based on the number of times an

5

advert is clicked on.

What is Pay-Per-Click?

Pay-per-Click or PPC is when your Google Adwords Adverts appears as part of the results page, that Google's Search Engine or a Partner Web Site displays for a search result.
Ads for relevant words are shown as 'sponsored links' that you see on the right side of your screen or above the main search results.

You do not pay for the advert unless someone clicks on the advert ... so you *pay ... per click*.

For example, your advert could be shown on 100 search result listing pages, but if only 10 people click on the advert, you would only pay for those 10 clicks.

This makes a lot of sense for an advertiser, as an advertiser only want potential clients/customers clicking on adverts, not everyone that sees the advert.

It has one huge disadvantage and that is that a badly written Google advert can end up getting clicks that are just costing you money.
This is because the person had no interest in your offer, but the advert *indicated* that they *might* find something of interest.

Why Use Google AdWords?

The reason that AdWords advertising is so popular, are the many advantages it has over other online advertising methods and over most traditional advertising methods.

- Google AdWords **helps you to target your adverts** *specifically* to people who are looking for your products
  or services.
  This means that you can avoid showing your adverts to people who are not likely to purchase from you.

- Google AdWords **helps you reach people** who you would find it difficult to reach using traditional Advertising, such as newspapers.

  So, instead of looking for newspapers or television stations in far-away places, which can pose logistical issues, you just need to use the internet to advertise.

- Cost is another advantage of Google AdWords.
  Adwords are very cost-effective for businesses of all sizes.
  This is because you get to choose to pay for ad clicks or Cost Per Click (CPC) or you can pay for impressions or Cost Per Thousand) CPM.

  Since you get to decide your own CPC or CPM amounts and your budget, the amount you pay each time someone clicks or views your ad is up to you. Once you set your budget correctly, you can't spend too much.

- Timing is another advantage of Google AdWords adverts since they allow you to **engage potential customers at precisely the right moment** — when surfers are actively searching for information (using keywords) related to your business.
  Your Google AdWords adverts ensure that your Web site is only a click away.

- With Google AdWords, there is **flexibility and control** in that you can edit an existing advert and you can edit your account, at any time and as regularly as you want.
  Your Google AdWords account is available 24 hours a day, 7 days a week, all year round. This makes setting up Seasonal advertising campaigns very easy.

- Yet another advantage is that Google **AdWords start running for the first time, almost immediately after you activate your account**. This has huge advantages for testing & research, as you can know very quickly if a new idea has potential.

- With traditional methods of advertising, you are expected to make payment before the Ad is put up. However, with Google AdWords, (*in most countries*) **you can decide to pay once a person has clicked on**

your Ad and so you are assured that the money you have used to advertise has served its purpose.

- With Google AdWords, **you can do conversion tracking**, which is very hard to do through traditional means, as knowing just how many people read your adverts on newspaper, television, etc, is difficult.
  With Google AdWords, you will be able to track the number of impressions or 'hits' an advert gets.

- Google AdWords **attract highly qualified visitors and your adverts will only appear to those who are searching for the targeted keywords.** So you can be sure that the visitors or traffic will be highly qualified and/or targeted, if you do your Keyword Research correctly.

Reasons Businesses Should Use Google AdWords

#1 Free Search Engine traffic can often dry up overnight, but Google AdWords is consistent. For a business owner, relying only on free search engine traffic is a big mistake because what the search engines give you, the search engines can take away.

This can be proven by the infamous 'Florida Update', that Google performed on its search engine results in 2003, which resulted in many web sites with perfect natural rankings being dropped from the search results.

This has happened many times since, at least every six months and the effects can be devastating for businesses that relied solely on the free search engine results from Google and did not use a Search Engine Optimization professional .

If they had been using Google AdWords, this problem would have been minimized, as their Adwords would still be showing and the Adwords Campaign could be updated to include any keywords you no longer show up for in the free listings.

#2 If you do not develop a Google AdWords campaign, your can be sure that your competitors will.

On each page of Google search results, there is usually space for between eight and ten Google AdWords ads. This means that eight to ten of your competitors have the chance to be on Google's first page. If they are not there now, they soon will be.

#3 Google AdWords provides excellent intelligence about the type, number and profitability of the words getting you more business..

Your Google Account contains data about your Campaign that enables the precise tracking of the effectiveness of each word or phrase you use in your campaign.

From this information, you can determine what the most frequently searched words are, what the highest converting words are and much more helpful information.

It can basically tell you which adverts are doing best, which helps you to know where to spend your advertising budget.

You can then use this information for SEO (Search Engine Optimization), which is the process of getting your website highly ranked in the natural (free) search engine results.

#4 Google AdWords can help establish a good key performance indicator benchmark.

An example of this is that you can use the cost of Adwords to determine an amount that you need to pay for each visitor on your website and also how much you need to pay for each lead or sale you make.

You can use these figures to compare all of your other website traffic sources against so as to determine just how effective they are.

#5 A Google AdWords campaign can help to rapidly drive traffic to your web site.. Using Search Engine Optimization, (SEO), it can take months before natural search engine traffic arrives at your web site.

A Google Adwords campaign can be started in a few days and only takes a few weeks to optimize.

So the speed advantage of Google AdWords, enables you to test new ideas rapidly to determine if there is a ready market for them.

#6 With Google AdWords, you can **level the demand** for your services by turning the Google AdWords campaign on and off as is necessary.
Since your Google AdWords campaign can be turned on or off in seconds, you have a tap for your website traffic.

This is beneficial, if you are inundated with orders or work and you cannot fulfill anymore at the moment, you just can turn off the AdWords traffic to your website, to delay further orders, until you are able to handle more work.

#7 The **precise targeting** feature of Google AdWords means that it is possible to target geographically and by language..

An example of geographically would be that you can have your AdWords adverts appearing for people searching from;

Manhattan, New York City, New York State,
a mix of New York City Boroughs
all of New York City,
all of New York State,
parts of New York State,
or the whole of the USA, in just a few minutes.

You can also target by language, which would mean that you could do the same as above, but only target people that Speak Spanish.

You can do the same worldwide, targeting only the countries that you want to advertise in.

#8 It is also possible to **target by time**.

As an example, if you wish, you can have your Google AdWords ads appear from 6:00 AM until 10 PM during weekdays, but 6:00 am until 12 midnight at weekends.

You could also do a targeted time Sale Campaign, for example, to follow the Super Bowl, that starts when the game begins and ends when the game ends.

What are "Keywords"?

Understanding the Power of Keywords, is probably THE must important key to marketing successfully on the Internet.

Keywords, simply put, are the words a person types in to a search engine to try to find what they are looking for. The word "Key" is key used as an adjective, in the context of *essential, important, crucial* or *decisive*.

There are what I call *obvious* keywords & *not so obvious* keywords. You need to take both into account.

So for example, if you were looking for a hotel in Rome, you might type "hotel in Rome" into Google.com. This would give you the Google results for Hotels in Rome, so *hotel in Rome* would be considered an **obvious** keyword for hotel owners in Rome.

If you were a Dentist, toothache, filling, cosmetic dentistry, etc would be some of the obvious keywords that you may want to use.

However from my experience, the **not so obvious** keywords, often generate you more profit for a business, as they can match what the Searcher is looking for exactly.

Lets take our example above of the Hotel Owner in Rome and show a not so obvious keywords that has the potential to do well.

With the Hotel example, if the hotel was near the Vatican, and people were typing "hotel near the

Vatican" into Google, then that phrase would be a not so obvious phrase to set up in Google Adwords for a few reasons.

1. Since the hotel is near the Vatican, it matches the location that the person was looking for.

2. As the person is specifying a location, it has been shown in research that they are further along the buying cycle and therefore more likely to book the hotel immediately.

3. Less competition in Google Adwords, as you would only be competing against hotel near the Vatican, not the whole of Rome.

4. That phrase may give you a far better Return On Investment, as it would probably cost you less per click and you would probably get a better sales percentage.

For all of these, when you do the keyword research that I show later in the book, each word that appears to be getting a lot of clicks and/or impressions, would do best when tested in detail.

What are YOUR keywords?

Choosing keywords to use with Google AdWords advertising is one of the most important, but difficult problems a marketer will face.

Think about it, if you know the words people use to find what they want in your Market, you can help them find it on your Website.

Note: There is a Local Business product from Google called Google Express that is a Done For You system, but it is still good to know how to find keywords, as this is the lifeblood of an Adwords Campaign.

Using the right keywords is crucial, so how do you figure out what words to use?

The first step is to find out what you think your keywords are. get your self a pen & paper. Write the name of the product or service in the middle of a sheet of paper and around this name, write down the first words and phrases that come to mind, connecting those words to the original word with a short line.

As we used this example already, let's say you are a dentist.
You should ask yourself, *"If I was a member of the Public, looking for something dentistry related, what would I type into a search engine?"*

Words like, *dentist ... emergency dentist ... filling ....*
tooth ache ... would probably etc. etc.

Do this for all the keywords you originally had on your
piece of paper, dig deeper on each keyword.
Write out as many as you can, take at least twenty
minutes brainstorming.

The next step is to use all the keywords you found as a
starting point, to build the Keyword list you are going
to use for your Google Adwords Campaigns, and here
is the tool I recommend you use.

The Google Adwords Keyword Tool

Google helps you to build a large list of keywords with
its Google Adwords Keyword Tool and you can find it
here,
https://adwords.Google.com/select/KeywordToolExternal.

This tool will tell you the different Keywords people
actually use, when searching in Google, during the
previous month. It will also show you roughly how many
competitors there are for each of these keywords *if* you
were going to use Google Adwords.

This is very good information to have, as if people are
spending a lot of money on a certain keyword, it follows
that they are probably making money from using that
keyword.

NOTE: Keywords with a lot of competition should each
go into a separate individual Adwords "Group", so that
you can test them and not blow your budget.

Start your list looking for the keyword terms with the least competition and the most monthly searches, as well as the obvious keywords that you know you have to use.

The Final Step in Keyword Research

Finally, you need to try to think like a potential Client, instead of an advertiser. Consulting family, friends and existing customers is always a good idea to get an average person's take on keywords.

Just ask them, *"If you were looking for my service / product in Google , what would you type in to the Search Box"*.

Don't dismiss any of the words.

You may think that a keyword is irrelevant, but YOU are not your Client, they may not know any of the common industry words.

Doing this can give you a whole new insight into how your potential customer actually goes looking for your service/ product on the Internet.

IMPORTANT: Now go back to the start of this section and use the Keyword Tool to do your final research for all the new keywords you found.

Keywords & Google Trends

Google Trends is another Google tool that allows you to see volumes of the most popular search words and phrases people are carrying out using Google.
This can be broken down geographically from worldwide to local cities or towns and allows you to compare hot search terms and their volumes.

Use your keyword list to research Trends and if you find that there is a popular search term that is relevant to your business, or in which you can find some connection, then you may be able ride the wave of it. You set up a test Adgroup for that keyword & monitor the results.

Alternatively, you can find popular search terms with a little less volume where the cost of showing ads next to them might be considerably cheaper.

There is also a service known as Google Trends for Websites that gives you a rough estimate on how popular particular websites are and allows you to compare them to most other websites broken down by geographic location.

This is an excellent way to gauge how popular your site is compared to that of your competitors or to find out which other sites are visited by the same target market that visits your site.

Utilizing the full power of Google Trends, does, however, take some experience. It is important to know how to extract and use the data provided and how to conduct keyword research that will allow you to ride a hot trend without getting your fingers burned financially.

When it comes to website comparison, you again need to know what to do with the information you have gained. Ideally, you need to be able to use it to tweak and target your own website and marketing campaign so that it works ever more efficiently for you.

Always use a separate Google Adwords Adgroup for keywords that you find in Google Trends, so that you don't end up spending money on a keyword that brings no sales.

Focus -
The Google Adwords Secret

It is important to break down your main keyword lists into smaller lists, (Adgroups), that are focused around subtopics. If your ads are not targeted precisely to your keywords, people may not click on your Google AdWords adverts.

You should make sure that the Adwords Advert persuades the Searcher that the page they will go to after clicking on the Ad, will hold the answer to what they are looking for,
So …. you need to make sure that page that the Advert send the searcher to when clicked, (called a Landing Page), **does** hold the answer to what they are looking for.

Your Google Adwords Landing Page

The **landing page** is where people that click on your Google AdWords adverts will be taken after a click. It's therefore important that this page be what the advert promised, otherwise you will not be able to convert as many clicks to sales and you will also get a bad Quality Score.

If your landing pages are done correctly, they should be good enough to also rank well in the organic (free) search engine listings.

The Internet gurus know to spend as much time developing the landing page, as they do on the Google

Advert that drove their visitors to that page in the first place – this is another key to Google Adwords success.

Try not to offer escape routes, that allow the visitor many options to get side-tracked. It's all right for your landing pages to have some similarities to the rest of the site's interface.

However, they don't have to be exactly the same, they can serve as stand-alone pages that funnel visitors to the desired call to action.

You should never take anything for granted. What is obvious to you, may not be so obvious to your visitors … test … test … test.

You should test multiple landing pages. Very few people go to the trouble of setting up more than one landing page to test different variables.

To get the most benefit from testing landing pages, use Google website Optimizer, http://www.google.com/websiteoptimizer/

Two points to note, taken directly from Google Adwords guidelines are ,Is your business and contact information easy to find? and Are you upfront about any information you're collecting from visitors?

Make sure that every landing page you make answers these questions.

Landing Page Gold

Taking the Dentist example again, if you had a Google Adwords advert for the keyword phrase *"emergency dentist"*, the page that this Advert send the searcher to when clicked should be about your *"emergency dentist"* service, NOT your home page or Contact Page

Here's Why!

If you give the person what they were looking for, you are far more likely to get a sale.

Here is an example of what a dentist should do.
The page should be tightly focused only on *emergency dentist.* It should have no clutter, it should show an office hours and an after office hours emergency telephone number, in big bold type.

It could also show a Google Map of the office location and driving directions that can be printed out. To give the visitor an extra push, it could contain a link that that can put into their smart phone, that brings them to the *emergency dentist* page of your Mobile web site.

You do have a Mobile web site?

Can you see how this works? A person looking for an emergency dentist comes to the page, straight away they see;

1. This is an emergency dentist
2. here is the phone number
3. here is where his office is
4. here are the directions

5. here is all the information on my mobile, so I can now leave for the Dentist immediately.

Are they going to keep searching or make that call?

As long as you have done your Geographic targeting correctly, that searcher was local, so they will make that call.

Think about what your potential clients/customers actually want and give them what they want, it will reward you very quickly in profits.

Match Types

There are special Match Type settings for each keyword that help control how closely the keyword needs to *match* a person's search term in order to trigger your ad.

There are four main Match Types, Broad Match, Phrase Match, Exact Match & Negative Match.

Broad match allows your Google ad to show for searches on similar phrases and relevant variations.

You add these keyword by just typing the keywords into the Add Keywords window..

Example: If you used the keyword Puppies

Your advert would show up for searches like: puppies , puppy photos, adopt a puppy, puppies food.

Phrase match allows your ad to show only for searches that include the exact phrase, or close variations of that exact phrase, and possibly other words as well.

You add these keyword by using " & " before & after the word.

Example: "adopt a puppy"

Your advert would show up for searches that can include: adopt a puppy, adopt a puppy, how to adopt a puppy

Exact match allows your ad to show only for searches that use that exact phrase, or close variations of that exact phrase, and no other words.

You add these keyword by using [&] before & after the word.

Example: [adopt a puppy]

Search that can match: adopt a puppy, adopt a puppy.

Negative match ensures that your ad doesn't show for any search that includes that term.

Example: -free

Searches that won't include: free puppy adoption, free puppy calendars, who wants to free the puppies

You can read more information about Matches from Google Adwords Support.

AdWords Costs

With Google AdWords, it is you who decides how much your adverts will cost. You get to set the price you pay each time a potential customer clicks on your ad, and you set a budget that limits how much you spend overall per day.

This does not mean you can get potential clients for a few cents, as you will still need to see what others are paying and decide if you want to pay more to get a better positioned advert, all will be explained below.

So, how much does a click really cost?

Well, Google AdWords is somewhat like an auction, where individual advertisers decide what a click is worth to them and then bid for it.

It is those bids, together with other factors like the Quality Score of adverts, discussed earlier, that are used to determine which Ad will appear and in each placement. , (i.e. 1st , 2nd , 3rd etc.)

With Google AdWords, you have 2 bidding options and these are that you can set your own maximum click price yourself or you can let the AdWords Budget Optimizer, a program by Google , set your bids to try and find you the most clicks possible within your budget.

When you create a Google AdWords account, Budget Optimizer is automatically enabled. I would recommend that *you switch off Budget Optimizer* and learn from experience.

When you decide to set your own maximum PPC, you might decide to pay as little as 10 US cent, ($0.10), each time a visitor clicks your advert.

You can also decide to pay one US dollar or much more for each click. Obviously, with a very low bid, your advert may not show very often, but with a very high bid, your advert may show up a lot. or too much.

As an illustration, it follows that if you set a price of $0.10 per click and your advert is clicked 25 times in a day, then your total charges for that day would be US$2.50.

Similarly, you might set a total monthly budget of just a few dollars, or as much as US$5,000 a month, or even more.

For example, if you were to set a monthly budget of US$30, (about a dollar daily), then your advert will be halted each day after it collects a dollar's worth of clicks.

You have the option of changing your pay per click and your budget at any time - even several times a day if you so choose.

There is no long-term contract or minimum spending limit for Google AdWords. You can even pause or suspend your campaign at will, which basically mean your Ads will stop showing and won't generate any new charges.

Your Google AdWords Ads will compete with Ads from other advertisers who have also set their own prices.

Your success will be based on how much you bid, the

quality of your adverts, how many other people want to advertise on the same keywords or key phrases, and other factors, especially the Quality Score.

You can always get a rough idea of costs and traffic for certain keywords by using Google's Traffic Estimator. Google AdWords should never be seen as just an expense, but instead as an investment, which returns more than you put in.

Calculating Return on Investment

Since any advertising is only effective if it generates measurable results for the business, your Google AdWords Advertising ROI or Return On Investment should be calculated regularly.

ROI can be calculated, by subtracting your advertising costs, from your sales revenue, dividing this by the cost of advertising and then multiplying this by 100 to convert it into a percentage.

For example, if your advertising costs for one week were, US$500 and you have made a profit US$1,000 dollars on sales from this, you 100 percent ROI for the week.

(*Subtracting 500 from 1000 and dividing this by 500 US dollars and then multiplying this by 100 to convert it into a percentage.*)

Determining your Google AdWords ROI can be a very straightforward process. You will already have access to the *advertising costs* for any specific time period for your Google AdWords account in your "Campaign Summary" statistics.

If you track your Adwords based sales, (by using separate landing pages & payment pages or codes, you can get your Sales Revenue.

NOTE

To help you track Adwords based sales, you should learn how to use Google Analytics, http://www.google.com/analytics/

You should also learn to set-up *Goals* within Google Analytics to monitor any Actions that you consider to be *Conversions*.

Conversions are when a user completes an action on your site, such as buying something or requesting more information, anything that you consider a good result.

What To Use As A Budget?

Google has explained budgeting in detail, in their help section, so it's worth reading that information.

The main rules are;

1. Know what you are prepared to spend to acquire a new client/customer.

2. Always be watching return on investment. When you start, you should do this daily, but once you are more confident that one keyword won't take all your budget & get you no new business, you can review weekly.

3. Decide how much you are going to spend and **stick to it.** Decide on your total yearly or monthly budget. Break that down to per day & stick to it.

A budget planner is also a good thing to start. Budget planning is essential to any marketing, because it will help you understand where your money has gone, however, budget plans are worthless if you don't stick to them.

At the end of the day, you need to know how much you have in the bank and how much you are willing to spend.

How is Your Google AdWords Ads Display Position Determined?

Google uses a unique method to determine position of your Google AdWords adverts on its site. They use a two-tier system to decide positioning of your Google AdWords adverts.

Your ranking on the Google AdWords is a function of the maximum *Cost Per Click*, your *Quality Score* and the *Click Through Rate* of each advert.

The highest bidder will not automatically be at the topmost (first) position on Google AdWords, as Quality Score and Click Through Rate are consider more important than how much an advertiser is willing to pay.

If any two advertisers have the same ranking of Google AdWords, the company determines your position by calculating as many numbers of decimal places as necessary.

Maintaining your position on the Google AdWords, basically depends on your *Click Through Rate* which means that if your advertisement records many clicks, you get to keep your position. However, if the click rate falls below the levels that Google has specified, you lose your position and ranking on the Google site.

However, improving your Quality Score can move you up the rankings, so a competitor could pass you out by doing this, so you should review your rankings at least weekly.

How The Google AdWords Winning Bidder Is Decided

The Google AdWords winning bidder, is determined by **Ad Rank,** not by maximum bid.

The Google AdWords system that determines who wins the Pay-per-Click auction, is based upon the belief that high quality adverts are of benefit all parties involved, which means they benefit Google, the advertiser and the Internet Surfers who will see the Google AdWords.

The winning bidder gets the highest position and the highest position gets the most clicks.

The goal for you, as a Google Adwords advertiser, is to get the best ROI (Return On Investment) for your advert, at the lowest possible cost per click (CPC).

Google ranks the triggered ads by 'Ad Rank' every time a search is done and an auction has taken place. The position of each advert is based on this 'Ad Rank' which is calculated as,

Ad Rank = Maximum Cost-per-Click x Quality Score.

Google assesses and measures the *relevancy* of your advert using the Quality Score and as seen from the formula above, this has a major effect in deciding how much you actually pay for every click.

What is Quality Score?

The ordering that the Adwords Adverts are shown, (i.e. 1st , 2nd , 3rd etc.) depends on many factors, the obvious one is how much other advertisers bid.
However, the most important factor is the 'Quality Score' of each advert that wants to be shown, for a given keyword.

The Quality Score is calculated using a variety of factors and measures how *relevant* your keyword is to your Adwords Ad Group, to a user's Search Query (keyword) and to the Landing Page for that advert.

It takes into account, the *relevance* of an Adwords advertiser's Ad text and keywords, the performance of each Advert (e.g. historical click-through rates), the advertiser's account history, and other relevance factors that only Google know.

Quality Score even determines if a keyword is eligible to enter the advert *auction* that occurs when a user enters a search query and also how high the advert will be ranked if this happens.

This Quality Score is also used by the Google to set the *minimum bids* for an advertiser's keywords.

The *minimum bid* also takes into account the *quality* of the landing page, which includes the originality and relevancy of the content, navigation on the web page, and transparency into the nature of the venture.

By transparency into the nature of the venture, I mean that if your web page has plenty of contact information, a mailing address, e-mail address, telephone number, Google likes it, but if you seem to be trying to hide your contact information, you raise suspicion with Google , so this can effect how much Google makes you pay.

Although Google has released a list of full guidelines for Websites to use, the precise formula and Google's definition of *relevance* can and actually does change regularly, as Google make improvements to their system.

It therefore follows that the higher your Quality Score is, the lower your advertising costs and the better your advert position.

Also, if your keyword has a low Quality Score, your advertising costs per keyword will be much higher and your advert position will be low.

Types Of Google Adwords Adverts

Google Adwords Text Ads

Google Adwords Text Ads are the links on the right side of the page and sometimes the Top of the page, displaying search results, where it says 'Sponsored Links'.

They use a method called Pay Per Click (PPC) advertising, where you only pay Google, each time your advert is clicked on.

You have the option of indirectly deciding where on the page your ad will appear, based on the keyword cost & quality score, as discussed already.

Google Adwords text Ads are short and are made up of,

- One title line of 25 characters, including spaces

- Two content text lines, of 35 characters each, including spaces

- A Display URL of 35 characters, including spaces

- A Destination URL, up to 1024 characters

Title Line

The Title line should be used like a Headline. it should have something in it to catch attention & definitely should have the keyword that you are using in it.

Second Line

The second line is your chance to show a Benefit, offer a solution, or ask a question that will qualify the person as someone that *should* be interested in your product or service.

Third Line

On the third line, make an offer, make a promise, solve a problem or ask for action, to further qualify the person.

Display URL

The display URL should be the address of the website that you're promoting. It is not the link to the landing page, but it can be the same URL, if there is enough space for it.

Do make it easy to read by capitalizing the first letter of each word and you can leave out the "www.", to get you more space.

If space will allow you, use "/" after the .com and add your keyword.

e.g. YourWebSite.com/keyword

Destination URL

The Destination URL is the address of the landing page, the only requirement is that it must be the same website as the Display URL.

So if the Display URL is the web site YourWebSite.com, the destination URL must also be on YourWebSite.com, but it can be any page on the website. Do remember to make that page a unique landing page for the keyword you are using in the advert.

Google Adwords Image, Audio and Video Ads

Google also offers Image Ads, Audio Ads (radio advertising) and Video Ads.
These types of Google Adverts are too specialized to be covered in this Book, but Google publishes plenty of information about using them, a quick look in Google Help will answer any questions.

Also, Google themselves will do all they can to get you started, keep an eye out for a contact telephone number once you get to the sign up page.

However, the same rules apply for all Google Advertising, Relevancy & Focus are the golden rules. If you want to do any Image, Audio or Video advertising with Google, keep your Target Market tightly focused for each Ad group.

Google Display Network

http://www.google.com/ads/displaynetwork/

Google also gives you the option of displaying your Ads on Content Sites in the ever growing **Google Network**. In these contents sites, you get to choose exactly where you want your Ad to be placed.

There is also an option of **Contextual Targeting** which matches your keywords to content, which is part of Google Network.

The Google Network

Google Network is divided into the **Search Network**, that includes Google itself and other search sites like AOL.com and into the **Display Networks**, Google sites (like YouTube, Blogger, and Gmail).

Since search results pages make up a very small fraction, about five percent, of all pages viewed on the Internet, Google Network provides a cheap way to reach users on the greater portion of the Internet.

To get the best out of in Google AdWords, you should also use the Google Network.

Most Adwords experts would recommend setting up an Adwords campaign specifically for the Google Network, so that budgets and keywords can be optimized specifically for the Network.

AdWords Language & Location Targeting

The importance of Customized Targeting cannot be over emphasized, especially if you are advertising locally. To access this option, look for "Locations and Languages" in your AdGroup settings and select Advanced Search

The three options are:

- **Entering a physical address** where you enter a street or business address.
  A distance can be chosen and this forms the radius over which users in the radius or those that include in their search the names of towns and cities within this circle will see the adverts.

- **Selecting a point on the map** where the center of the advertising circle can be defined by dragging the interactive map to place a red marker on your location.
  It is this location that will automatically be converted to exact latitude and longitude coordinates which the Google AdWords system will use to target your ads.

- Finally, **multi-point targeting** lets an advertiser click 3 or more points on an interactive map to outline the advertising region where they want their Ads to appear.
  The Google AdWords system will convert the points you select to latitude and longitude automatically. Using this method of targeting, business owners or individuals can create target areas of virtually any size and shape.

Using Google Analytics to monitor your progress

Tracking how your Ads are performing is important in determining what works and what doesn't.
With proper data, you can make a more informed decision about how to adjust your advert text, keywords, and bids so that you can be more successful in your marketing campaign.

Google Analytics is free of charge to anyone who wants to monitor traffic. It's easy to install and all you need is to paste a few lines of HTML text, which Google provides, into any web page that you want to monitor traffic.

These few lines of HTML text, sends information to your Google Analytics account, when a person visits your Web page.
Google Analytics then stores all this information, so that you can view it and see how visitors found your site and what they did while on your web site.

Note: Only you can view your Google Analytics data, because only you can log into your Google Analytics account and people cannot insert their own Google Analytics HTML into your Web page because they cannot log into that either.

One important function of Google Analytics is a finding out which keywords or key phrases are working and which are not.

Google Analytics shows;

- The number of visitors on a daily basis over a period of time that you have specified
- The number of page views

- The average time each visit takes
- The countries of origin of your visitors

- The city of origin of your visitors (in some regions only.)
- The number of new visitors and repeat visitors

- The search engines that visitors to your site have used
- The keywords and key phrases used by visitors to find your site

- The average number of pages viewed in every visit
- The bounce rate

In summary, Google Analytics is an important tool that gives various layers of understanding about how, why, and for whom their site is, or is not performing.

Google AdWords Tips & Tricks

You should always be specific when choosing your keywords, because using general keywords in your adverts, will bring lots of clicks to your website but not many actual buyers.
In other words the conversion rate will be very low and your Return On Investment (ROI) will be less.

You should use **Exact Match**, (*square brackets "[ ]" around the keywords*) of the keyword phrases that you want to target the most.
By doing this, your adverts will be shown only when searches are made that exactly match your keywords or phrase. You can gradually expand the Match types you use.

You should **offer the benefits** that your product or service will give in the advert, not features.

You should always **make multiple adverts**.
Make a copy an advert and make one change to it, so that you have two almost identical adverts.
With constant monitoring of your ads, you will be able to see which one is better. Then change the lesser responsive ad, to try another version of the better advert.

You should **record the return on investment** or ROI of all adverts to keep your expenses within your pre-decided budget and update or change low ROI adverts. ROI should be the main decider when planning adverts.

You should **test using words that have been proven to**

increase clicks, like *free, free shipping, limited time offer & special offer*.

You should always break your keyword down into **tightly focused Adgroups**, with as few keywords as possible in each group.
Yes, this takes time, but you will get the benefit later when you can see at a glance, which Adgroups are doing very well and with less keywords to test, it is easier to find the keywords responsible for sales.

You should **set spending limits** (budget) so that you don't go overboard. Google AdWords gives you the ability to set daily spending limits for keywords and you should use this feature to control the cost of your adverts.

Disadvantages of Google AdWords

Just like anything in life that has pros, Google AdWords have some cons too.

The major disadvantage is the failure rate of Google AdWords campaigns, caused by the sharp learning curve. This means it takes a long time to learn all the strategies necessary to build a profitable campaign.

During the first few months of the campaign, you may end up spending more than you are making.
If you have a daily budget of 100 dollars at 2 dollars per click and easily receive 50 clicks that give no sales, you will already have spent 100 dollars on the first day.

Google even assesses how well or how badly you *organize* your campaigns, and this effects your quality score.
If you have a low quality score, Google will increase the minimum bid you have to pay for your keywords.

Although Google AdWords campaigns are easy to set up, many people fail to track their keywords and so they never know exactly which keyword triggered the sale and exactly which keywords get clicks, (*which cost you money*), but no sales.

Google makes suggestions such as suggesting that you should pay more, and this may not always the best action to take. Look at your budget and decide yourself.

Google also have an automatic matching feature that turns on automatically and I strongly recommend that you opt out of this. You can always test it later.

With Google AdWords, you can lose money fast if you don't know how it works.

> Get more **free** Digital marketing help, go to http://www.eoinoleary.com/book-bonus/
>
> The information there will change regularly, as I keep it up to date. Expect to find articles, videos & webinars, all free to you .... but with a real value of at least US$200.

Conclusion

Google AdWords are an important advertising tool and this can be seen from the amount of money that it brings the company.

Starting a Google AdWords campaign is not easy, but with the right information, anyone can do it, if they take the time to learn.

Google AdWords work on an auction-based system that assigns particular words and interested parties place bids for them.

Quality Score is a vital part of getting Google Adwords right, it determines if a keyword is eligible to enter the advert, how high the advert will be ranked and how much you pay for each person that clicks on your advert.

Having a successful Google AdWords campaign requires good landing pages.

Google has tools that help you to determine what to bid for an Ad, however, you should never go beyond your budget.

Tracking how your Google AdWords adverts are performing is important in determining what works and what doesn't.

Google Analytics is a free tool provided by Google to anyone who wants to monitor traffic, and you should use it.

Eoin O'Leary

Resources

The Google AdWords Learning Center

The Google AdWords Learning Center contains a huge list of How To videos and also links to Adwords Support for any questions that you may have.
http://www.google.com/ads/learn/

Adwords Express

AdWords Express is a new form of advertising available for Local Business, it is basically Google AdWords on auto-pilot.

I haven't had enough feedback to recommend it and I also prefer to be able to test & track keywords to get the best Return On Investment, so I personally think that it would end up costing the business owner more in the long run.
http://www.google.com/adwords/express/

Google Adwords Editor

This is a tool from Google that you can download that makes making your Adwords Campaigns far easier.

It does so much that I think it would be better for you to just take a look for yourself.
http://www.google.com/intl/en/adwordseditor/

About The Author

I have been involved in Digital Marketing since 1994, back when there was email & not much else and I learned what I could from the limited information available at the time.

After being a director in two start-up Small Businesses in early 2000, I could see that Marketing was the life blood of any company and that Internet Marketing was the future.

It was then I began to take a far more serious interest in learning Internet Marketing, spending over US$18,000 on courses, books & seminars.

In 2009. I became a Qualified Google Advertising Professional and I now specialize in helping Small Business Owners get more clients for their business.

I work with a limited number of Small Business Owners that sell a service, to help them maximize the return on investment for their Digital Marketing.

However, I don't believe in using Google Adwords alone, I believe in using all available methods to build a businesses profits.

I see it like deciding to build a house, but not spending money on doors & windows. Yes, you will get some benefit from four walls and a roof, but you will always know that you should have done better when times get tough.

51

If you want to contact me about the possibility of working with you, just go to www.eoinoleary.com and get on my Private mailing list.

I take clients on a first come first served basis and if there is an opening to work with me, the first step is a Profit Improvement Strategy Session, so that I can see what methods will benefit your business.

Why not go to my web site right now, waiting until later just means that you're getting further behind your competition, missing out on clients that could have been yours.

I hope you enjoyed this Book.

To you success

Eoin O'Leary

eoinoleary.com

P.S. Don't forget to get more free Digital marketing help, go to http://www.eoinoleary.com/book-bonus/